I0345651

A Guide to Keith Johnstone's

THEATRESPORTS™

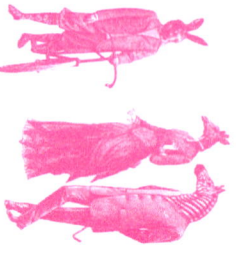

Published 2017 by the International Theatresports™ Institute (ITI)

215 - 36 Avenue NE, Unit 6 | Calgary, AB | T2E 2L4 | CANADA

Copyright © 2017 ITI

Originally produced exclusively for ITI performance rights members free of charge. Now also available to non-members.

This guide is in no way a replacement for performance rights. Non performance rights holders wishing to perform the Theatresports™ format should apply at: admin@theatresports.org.

Layout: Dagmar Bauer konzipiert & gestaltet, Stuttgart, Germany
Illustrations by fotolia.com

International Theatresports Institute

Cover Photograph:
Teatro A Molla - Bologna, Italy
📷 *by Gianluca Zamboni*

Photo next page:
Loose Moose Theatre - Calgary, Canada
📷 *by Breanna Kennedy*

CONTENTS

8 INTRODUCTION
- 8 About This Guide
- 9 Keith Johnstone
- 10 Resources
- 10 The International Theatresports™ Institute (ITI)

12 THEATRESPORTS™ BACKGROUND
- 12 What is Theatresports™?
- 12 Theatresports™ Origins
- 13 The Global Explosion of Theatresports™
- 15 What Theatresports™ Can Achieve
- 15 Content

16 IMPORTANT CONCEPTS
- 16 What You Need to Know Before You Start
- 16 The Spirit
- 17 Failure
- 18 Teamwork
- 18 Misbehavior
- 19 Skills
- 20 Terminology

22 LET'S BEGIN
- 22 Theatresports™ by Stealth
- 22 The Quick Start
- 23 What You Need for Basic Theatresports™
- 23 A Theatresports™ Show
- 24 The 10 Minute Game
- 25 The Free Impro
- 25 The Danish Game
- 26 The Regular Challenge Match
- 27 Variety

28 THEATRESPORTS™ IN MORE DETAIL
- 28 Disaster is Unavoidable
- 28 The Start of the Show
- 29 Commentator/Emcee
- 29 Competition
- 30 Teams
- 30 Team Entrances
- 31 Seating the Teams
- 31 Leaving the Stage
- 32 Judges
- 33 Judges Entrance
- 33 Hell Judges
- 34 The Horn
- 37 The Basket
- 37 Scoring and Scorecards
- 38 Fairness
- 38 Challenges
- 41 Winning Prizes
- 41 Keith's Advice

42 ATTENTION TO DETAIL
- 42 Scenography
- 43 Notes
- 44 Games List

46 IN CLOSING
- 46 Final Words
- 46 For More Information

INTRO- DUCTION

ABOUT THIS GUIDE

We hope you find this guide to be a useful resource for information and inspiration about how to play Theatresports™.

It has been created to provide assistance for groups just starting out, to give direction to those who are unsure if they are heading in the right direction, and as a reminder to groups who have been playing a long time to check in on their progress and development.

Here you will find information about the history of Theatresports™, the skills needed to play, the spirit and theory behind the concept, as well as practical information on the structure, the components and how to put them together in performing the format. Throughout you will find useful Keith Johnstone quotes, suggestions that might inspire discussion points with your group, and interesting Theatresports™ notes to aid you in successfully and enjoyably playing Theatresports™.

Vancouver Theatresports - Canada (ca. 1982)

Most of the material in this study guide comes directly from Keith Johnstone via his classes, newsletters, his writings about Theatresports™ in his book IMPRO FOR STORYTELLERS and through conversations with him personally. Additional material and commentary is provided by improvisers who have practiced Theatresports™ for decades and worked with Keith over the past 40 years. Some of them are, or have served as members on the board of the International Theatresports™ Institute (ITI).

Although there are insights here on improvisation, this guide is primarily focused on Theatresports™. We encourage you to continue building your improvisation skills through study with informed teachers and various resources, such as Keith Johnstone's:

Books
IMPRO Improvisation and the Theatre
(available in many languages)
IMPRO FOR STORYTELLERS
http://www.keithjohnstone.com/writing/
http://theatresports.com/keiths-books/

DVDs
Impro Transformations
Trance Masks
keithjohnstone.com/video/
theatresports.com/dvds-on-keith/

Workshops
Keith Johnstone Impro intensives
keithjohnstone.com
The Loose Moose Theatre International Summer School
loosemoose.com
Teachers from the ITI suggested teacher list
theatresports.com/teachers/
ITI member companies (some with training programs)
theatresports.org/our-members/

Enjoy your journey into the world of Theatresports™ and may you find the fun, inspiration, and great potential in the format that many thousands all over the globe have also found since 1977.

ITI – Inspire The Improviser!

Did you know?.... Theatresports™ has been played on every continent except Antarctica and in over 60 countries!

As an improviser, you are not trying to succeed all the time, you're performing risky actions in search of a miracle.

Don't do your best. Make the other people look good. Then you look good.

Make the mistakes and stay happy.

Keith Johnstone

KEITH JOHNSTONE

Keith Johnstone was born in 1933 in Devon, England. He grew up disillusioned by school, finding that it blunted his imagination. The Royal Court Theatre commissioned a play from him, and he continued to work there from 1956 to 1966, as a play-reader, director and drama teacher, ending as an Associate Director. In his classes he began to question the impact schooling had on his imagination by exploring the reversal of all that his teachers had told him in an attempt to create more spontaneous theatre actors. It was at this time that Keith developed a series of improvisational exercises to help playwrights overcome writers block and for actors to work more spontaneously. He founded the improvisation group The Theatre Machine in the 1960's, which toured Europe and North America and was invited by the Canadian Government to perform at Expo 67. Keith moved to Calgary, Alberta, Canada in the 1970's and in 1977 co-founded the Loose Moose Theatre Company.

Keith invented the Impro System and improvisation shows such as Gorilla Theatre™, Maestro Impro™, Life Game and Theatresports™. He is a Professor Emeritus of The University of Calgary. His books (IMPRO and IMPRO FOR STORYTELLERS) outsell Stanislavsky in Germany. He is a playwright of children's productions and both short and full-length adult plays which have been performed in Europe, North America, Africa and South America.

by Steve Jarand

Stanford University is home to The Keith Johnstone papers which consist of original plays, writings, correspondence, theatrical materials, journals, artwork, and more. To be more specific, it includes early chapter drafts of IMPRO and IMPRO FOR STORYTELLERS™ (inc. early writings & drafts on Theatresports™), some of Keith's original, letters (including letters to Keith from Del Close, Peter Coyote, Samuel Beckett, Harold Pinter, Anthony Stirling, Royal Court colleagues, Theatre Machine members, etc.). It also includes many of Keith's earliest short stories, documents from his years with Royal Court, Theatre Machine and Loose Moose Theatre plus newspaper clippings, reviews, programs, photos, letters, artwork, and posters.

INTRODUCTION

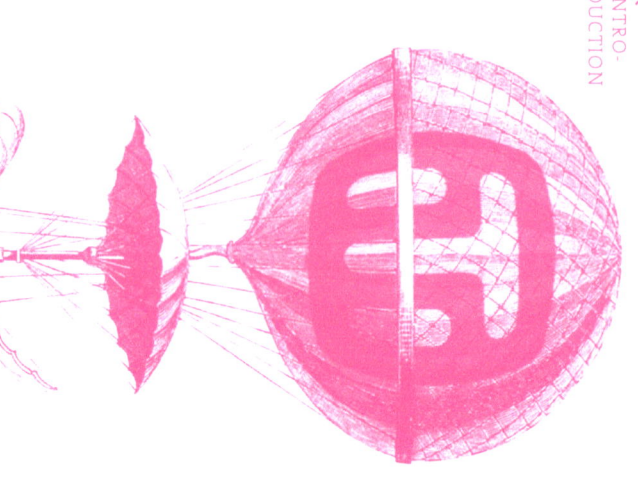

THE INTERNATIONAL THEATRESPORTS™ INSTITUTE (ITI)

In 1998, the International Theatresports™ Institute (I.T.I.) was created. It is a democratic organization to which Keith Johnstone has entrusted the legacy of the format Theatresports™. The ITI is a membership association of groups and individuals joined together by a shared passion in the work of Keith Johnstone.

The purpose of the ITI is:

1. To continue as the world's most reputable authority on Keith Johnstone's formats: Theatresports™, Gorilla Theatre™ and Maestro Impro™.
2. To create a lively, engaged and sharing community of members.

Those groups who perform one or more of the formats: Theatresports™, Maestro Impro™, and Gorilla Theatre™ do so after applying for and being approved for performance rights. Rights are extremely inexpensive and there are concessions for countries with a low GDP. Schools are also required to obtain permission but there are no fees attached. The ITI manages the licensing of the formats to these groups and provides resources for learning and development in the field of improvisation. Fees collected from performance rights go towards managing the ITI and giving support to its members. Keith Johnstone has always refused to take any money from Theatresports™ royalties. All Theatresports™ royalties go towards development and services for the ITI and its licensed groups.

The ITI is here to support you and answer any questions you may have regarding Keith's work including improvisation techniques, games and the use of the Theatreports™ itself. Please don't hesitate to contact us at: admin@theatresports.org.

Theatresports™ was the first form of international exchange in Improvisation. Groups from around the globe first spoke to each other through the common language of Theatresports™.
Randy Dixon - Unexpected Productions
Seattle, USA

RESOURCES

Biographical Information
Keith Johnstone -
A Critical Biography by Theresa Robbins Dudeck

The Keith Johnstone Papers
Questions about the "Keith Johnstone Papers" or inquiries about Johnstone's literary works, contact Theresa Robbins Dudeck, Literary Executor for Keith Johnstone.
trdudeck@gmail.com
theresarobbinsdudeck.com

It's called playing. It's a play. You're a player. Think of that.

Keith Johnstone

UWCSEA Theatresports Show - Singapore
with permission from UWCSEA

THEATRE-SPORTS™ BACKGROUND

WHAT IS THEATRESPORTS™?

Theatresports™ is an improvisation based theatre format and the artistic creation of Keith Johnstone. It entertains and educates the performers and audience. On the surface it is a team based 'theatre competition' with the same illusory struggle that professional wrestling exhibits. In front of the audience the competitors seem intent on winning, but inside them is a mutual desire to create dynamic, interesting theatre through spontaneity skills, storytelling and supportive play. Theatresports™ is capable of inducing laughter, tears, sport event style screaming and provoking thought, all while engaging and entertaining an audience.

Improguise - Capetown, South Africa
📷 *by Candice von Litzenberg*

THEATRESPORTS™ ORIGINS

*Loose Moose Theatre
Calgary, Canada
(ca. 1981)*
📷 *by Deborah Iozzi*

*Loose Moose Theatre
Calgary, Canada
(ca. 1981)*
📷 *by Deborah Iozzi*

Theatresports™ was inspired by pro-wrestling. The bouts took place in cinemas (in front of the screen) and the expressions of agony were all played 'out-front'. No theatre person could have believed that it was real. Wrestling was the only form of working-class theatre that I'd seen, and the exaltation among the spectators was something I longed for, but didn't get, from 'straight' theatre.

We fantasized about replacing the wrestlers with improvisers, an 'impossible dream' since every word and gesture on a public stage had to be okayed by her Majesty's Lord Chamberlain.

It was embarrassing to have visiting Russians commiserate with us over our lack of freedom.

I was giving comedy classes in public and the Lord Chamberlain was reluctant to open that can of worms, but Theatresports™ - a competition between teams of improvisers - could not be presented as 'educational'. It was just a way to liven up my impro classes until I moved to Canada.

Keith Johnstone - Impro For Storytellers pg. v/2

THE GLOBAL EXPLOSION OF THEATRESPORTS™

Keith was exploring the basis of Theatresports™ in his classes at the Royal Court Theatre in the late 1950's and testing it in front of audiences with his group The Theatre Machine around Europe in the 60's. Theatresports™, as we now know it, was first performed publicly in 1977 by a group of university students who later formed The Loose Moose Theatre Company in Calgary AB, Canada. It quickly became a phenomenon! Audiences couldn't believe what they were seeing. Fearless performers were taking huge risks and creating a show out of thin air. The energy in the theatre was electric and shows were selling out. Word of this new show started to spread and Theatresports™ companies began popping up all over. Keith's reputation and international teaching lead to a further spread of the form and soon Loose Moose Theatre would host an array of international guests wanting to learn more from Keith and more about Theatresports™. Many of these individuals brought Theatresports™ back to their countries and the explosion continued.

Due to the rapid and enthusiastic spread of the format, changes began to appear.

Keith Johnstone Impro For Storytellers pg 23

When Theatresports™ is played by people who've had minimal or zero contact with me, you may be seeing a copy of a copy - and with each step it will have become 'safer' and sillier.

As teaching is mostly an oral tradition, these adaptations occurred, at times, because of misinterpretation or lack of information. It makes sense that with the newness of the work, choices were made in an attempt to make things easier. The result of these choices, however, often reduced the risk of failure, a key component of Keith's work. Removing the risk changes the creative vision of the format.

For example, a few common changes were:
- replace scenes with games as the bulk of the content
- increase the focus on competition and remove the focus on theatre and story
- remove the horn
- make the Judges a part of the entertainment by dressing them in silly costumes or making them characters

Personal risk in the face of failure, narrative, and supportive play are essential elements of Theatresports™ and the Johnstone Impro System.

Those who play with modifications that alter the style of improvisation that Theatresports™ allows may be unaware of how they weaken the format. This is understandable as groups have often had a difficult time finding resources in which to learn from. Key questions of Why? and How? may not have been available to them.

This guide aims to help answer those questions and provide an understanding of the essential concepts of Theatresports™. We hope this information will inspire groups and individuals, regardless of experience, to re-connect with the creative aims of its original approach.

Improvisation Illegal?! Hard to believe but true!

Theatre was censored in Great Britain. Public performances of improvisation were illegal because there was no script to censor. There are still some improvisation companies dealing with government censorship.

THEATRESPORTS™ BACKGROUND

A Story From Australia

When we first played Theatresports™, the Impro training made sense, but the performances didn't. They failed to overcome the desire of humans to actually compete, instead of creating the best show possible, as part of an ensemble. There was no concept of judges 'taking heat', and being a part of that supportive ensemble and the MC used about half of the performance time, introducing the teams and scenes.

Then, after the period of initial hype, our audiences became less interested. Attendance numbers were going down and we realized the company needed to change something. Eventually we got some proper guidance and training about how to bridge the gap between the theoretical and practical. We began to understand the relationship with the audience and some of the strategies to sustain variety and discovery. There was now room in the show for new players and veterans, cushioned by a format that made them all look good …and we were able to play twice as many scenes in the same time frame!

Our performers loved playing, twice as much as before, and our audiences doubled, returning each year, when we hold our season. Oh, we have our own little local quirks, but now there's a solid foundation. Nick Byrne - Impro ACT, Canberra

I always start with mime tug of war, or no 'S' game when teaching competitive formats. Play up the competition onstage, it actually lessens the conflict between improvisors.

Jeff Gladstone - Vancouver Theatresports, Canada

Theatresports™ can be funnier and sometimes more significant than the copied versions. What matters is making things happen i.e. storytelling.

Storytelling and good nature and the expression of a point of view require skill. Getting on stage to play games based on audience suggestions is not much of an achievement, and is ultimately less satisfying to either performers or audience.

Keith Johnstone

Did you know…

With the explosion of Theatresports™ many cities were hearing that title before they had even heard the word improvisation. In some places around the world "Theatresports™" is still used interchangeably for the concept of "IMPROVISATION" itself. Not all improvisation is Theatresports™. "Improvisation" is the skill used in the show format of "Theatresports™".

Rapid Fire Theatre - Edmonton, Canada
by Marc-Julien Objois

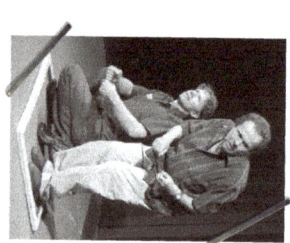

Loose Moose Theatre
Calgary, Canada
by Kate Ware

Teatrul National Gargu-Mures, Romania   by Christina Ganj

WHAT THEATRESPORTS™ CAN ACHIEVE

Keith Johnstone - Impro For Storytellers pg. 24

Theatresports™ can:
- Alleviate the universal fear of being stared at;
- Turn 'dull' people into 'brilliant' people (i.e. 'negative' people into 'positive' people);
- Improve interpersonal skills and encourage a life-long study of human interaction;
- Improve 'functioning' in all areas (as it says on the snake oil bottles).
- Develop story-telling skills (these are more important than most people realize);
- Familiarize the student with the bones of theatre as well as the surface;
- Give the stage back to the performers;
- Allow the audience to give direct input, or even to improvise with the performers, rather than sit trying think up intelligent things to say on the way home.

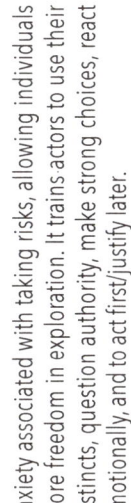

BATS, San Francisco, USA 📷 by Stephanie Pool

Over the decades, Theatresports™ and improvisation techniques associated with it have become useful tools for training performers and non-performers in areas of social interaction, group dynamics, creative thinking, public speaking, and leadership skills. It develops confidence and skills in writing/storytelling and communication. It strengthens co-operation and team building. It teaches the necessity of accepting mistakes and failure as a healthy component of a learning process and therefore reduces the anxiety associated with taking risks, allowing individuals more freedom in exploration. It trains actors to use their instincts, question authority, make strong choices, react emotionally, and to act first/justify later.

Leave your egos at home.
Shawn Kinley
Loose Moose Theatre,
Calgary, Canada

CONTENT

A common, and reasonable misinterpretation of Theatresports™ is that the show is focused mainly on performing Impro games. Actually, a Theatresports™ show may have few or no games. Improvisation is often taught through a series of games one could see in a Theatresports™ show, so thinking the main focus is to play these games can certainly be understood. Theatresports™, in fact, is an evening of improvised theatre & storytelling using sporting elements to generate a dynamic atmosphere for the audience. The games are added for variety and are not meant to be the bulk of the show content. It is common for companies who have worked with or been influenced by Keith to bring theatrical elements such as Masks and puppets onto the stage in improvised scenes or to explore elements such as movement, clowning and genuine emotion, or content focused on history, religion, society and current events. Theatresports™ is creating a different form of theatre.

Improv is scorching and everybody loves to see someone playing with fire.
Antonio Vulpio
Teatro a Molla, Bologna, Italy

IMPORTANT CONCEPTS

WHAT YOU NEED TO KNOW BEFORE YOU START

Theatresports™ will be a richer experience if you start by cultivating improvisational skills and the right spirit needed in approaching the format. Players need to learn to accept each other's ideas and to create stories. These building blocks apply in games or scenes; they are the foundation of the work. It is natural to want to remain safe which is why players are experts in protecting themselves from moving stories forward or allowing other characters/improvisers to have any control. Even though it is a mimed lion, improvisers will often respond to 'put your head in his mouth with a 'you first'.

The desire to play the show immediately is strong. You are encouraged, however, to read through the rest of the guide, consult with an ITI teacher, and read Keith Johnstone's writing directly. This will help gain understanding of each show component and how specifically designed choices serve the production and performance of Theatresports™.

THE SPIRIT

Keith's work is a specific style of improvisation technique and performance. The foundation of this work comes from understanding the spirit of the work. Aspects of the "spirit" include:

· Playfulness
· Supporting your partner and valuing their ideas
· Risk taking and bravery
· Honesty and vulnerability
· Being positive
· Failure - Learning to fail gracefully and good-naturedly
· Teamwork
· Misbehavior

Let's look deeper into the last three...

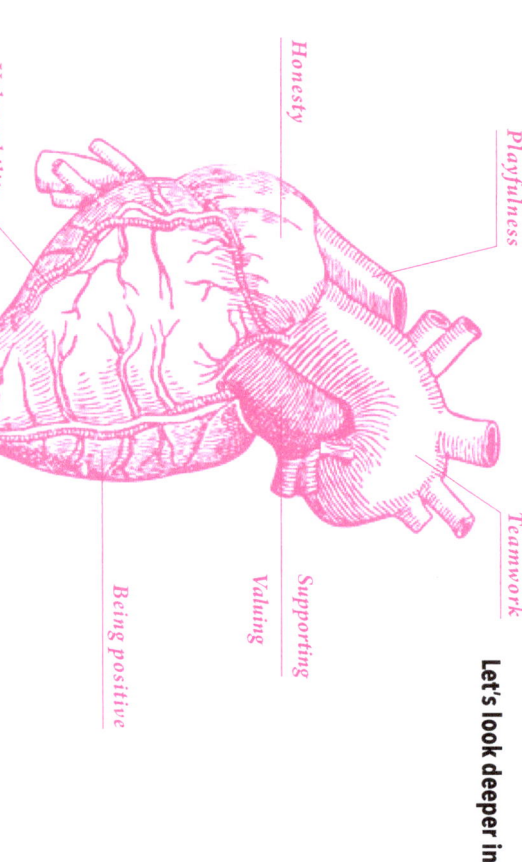

Vulnerability
Honesty
Playfulness
Teamwork
Supporting
Valuing
Being positive

FAILURE

In our society, failure is a concept laden with judgement and stress. Yet we know that through failure we learn; and in order to take a risk we need to be prepared for possible failure. In order for improvisers to play freely they must embrace failure and face risk. The result gives us the opportunity to show the audience a very special creature: the fearless, good-natured improviser who can stumble through crocodile filled pits and flames of hell and come out the other side with sparkles of joy still in their eyes, un-defeated by that which would bury the average person.

Keith Johnstone - Theatresports™ and Lifegame Newsletter - Issue Number 1, 1989

From the beginning of his training the student should be taught not to frown, not to tense up the muscles, not to sweat and moan and suffer when he fails. No one pays money to see that; we can get that at home.

Failure should be welcomed as an essential component of any game, and as an opportunity to show your generosity and good nature. Fail and stay happy and the audience think you're lovable and charming; they want to cuddle you and buy you drinks. Scowl, look pissed off and full of rage, and you seem detestable, spoiled, self centered and unsportsmanlike. I've seen Wimbledon Champions that I'd hate to be in the same room with; ill- humour and malevolence don't matter in tennis, but such behavior is a disaster in theatre where it doesn't really matter who wins, but where the spectators have got to have a good time, have got to relax and enjoy themselves and should love and admire the performers.

Keith Johnstone - Theatresports™ and Lifegame Newsletter - Issue Number 1, 1989

I used to think that I should try to prevent the student from ever experiencing failure – I thought I could do this by always selecting exactly the right material and by grading it in tiny steps. These days I think it is more important to teach ways of dealing with the pain of failure. I tell the students blame the teacher, laugh, never demonstrate a determination to try harder. The audience likes to see failure, but they don't like to see the performer punish himself.

The reason why so few people understand the value of failure, is that it is usually tied to horrible self-punishment which is nothing to do with learning (muscle tension probably makes learning more difficult) and is purely defensive.

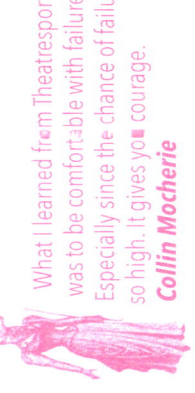

What I learned from Theatresports™ was to be comfortable with failure. Especially since the chance of failure is so high. It gives you courage.
Collin Mocherie

Theater Anundpfirsich, Zurich, Switzerland
📷 *by Mike Hamm*

TEAMWORK

Theatresports™ IS teamwork. Interestingly, it is often seen as one team in competition with another. In reality the team includes ALL of the performers, technicians, volunteers and audience. The battle is against boredom, safety and mediocrity. The victory holds a reward of fun, enthusiasm and strong, positive memories. Improvisation technique is built on teamwork. We accept and support each other's ideas so we can take creative risks. It doesn't make sense in a form grounded in supporting each other that we would abandon that in the performance. When one team refuses to help a competitor's scene, they might benefit themselves by winning one challenge but end up sending signals counter-productive to improvisation. It isn't about your individual glory, but a focus on working with each other to give the audience a good show. When a team jumps in to help the opposing team in aid of the show, the audience is rewarded with a benevolent experience. When the audience returns week after week because of quality performances, the players are rewarded with the success of the company.

Picnic Improvisación Teatral
Bogotá, Colombia
by Romina Cruz

MISBEHAVIOR

Connected to the spirit of the work, Keith always encouraged a balanced amount of misbehavior in the Theatresports™ format. He wanted the audience to see the players as "Happy, benevolent creatures, released from their cages" once a week, sometimes a little difficult to control. Play and misbehavior add to the experience as long as the misbehavior is in good spirit.

Mean spirited acts like put downs or serious arguments about the scoring of a scene is not in the interest of anyone except those with big egos. Misbehavior must not interfere with the show. It should add to the experience. Here are a few examples of inspired misbehavior:

A player "delays the game" by tweeting about how great the judges look or by taking their picture.

The improvisers (unceasingly) insist their fellow team members (not they) should have the honor to play the next scene.

One of the teams keeps starting extra scenes off to the side of the stage, attempting to have their own rebel show for a few special audience members.

> If misbehavior is understood, everyone becomes bolder. It works best if it is used to fill dead time. Avoid it and there will always be something slaveish about your work.
>
> Keith Johnstone Impro For Storytellers p. 20

SKILLS

It is not uncommon that an improvisation group may learn an oversimplified explanation of improvisation techniques. For example 'always say yes, never say no.' Acceptance of offers IS a key component however this isn't simply saying yes. We train in acceptance to encourage support so players can take creative risks without fear of judgement. Once this spirit is in place we then must look at how to build these ideas into stories for the audience. Skills such as being present, fearless creative risk taking, embracing failure, giving up control, total acceptance and support of others are suppressed in our daily lives and therefore take time to develop and maintain.

Here are some Impro fundamentals followed by related games/exercises from IMPRO FOR STORYTELLERS:

If you want to banter with the other team, act like you're suppressing laughter underneath.
Nils Petter Morland
Det Andre Teatret, Oslo, Norway

Don't do your best because it causes instant stage fright. When you see experienced improvisers (or mountaineers) doing their best it's because they're in trouble.
Keith Johnstone

Spontaneity/Present Moment:
Our fear of being judged and desire to be liked keeps us searching in our heads for what to do next. As improvisers we need to train how to be present; otherwise we don't see or hear what's happening, can't react honestly and won't be able to work with our partners.
· Wide Eyes – pg. 205/206
· Emotional Sounds – pg. 268-270
· Emotional Goals – pg. 184/185
· Hat Games – pg. 19, 156-161
· Mantras – pg. 270-274
· Sandwiches – pg. 236/237

Giving up Control
Also connected to fear, we try to control our body and minds then find that we've lost truthful emotion and physical relaxation. Exercises designed to take responsibility away from players in different ways can be liberating.
· Tug of War pg. 57/58
· Word at a Time – pg. 114-115, 131-134, 329
· One Voice – pg. 171-177
· He said/she said (Stage Directions) – pg. 195-199
· Dubbing (Synchro) – pg. 171-178
· Moving Bodies – pg. 200-202

Being Physical
Talking too much and explaining away our feelings and desires is a primary improviser defence. An alternative is to play physically so our bodies tell the stories instead of our intellect.
· Justify the Gesture – pg. 193-195
· Gibberish – pg. 185/186, 214-219
· Changing the Body Image – pg. 276-277
· People as Objects – pg. 303-304
· Sit/Stand/lie – pg. 366/367

Status
Status is a direct line towards relationship. We are playing status at every moment and to enhance or mess with it can reveal dramatic and fascinating human interaction.
· Various status exercises – pg. 219-231
· Master/Servant – pg. 240/241
· Making Faces – pg. 162-168
· Pecking Orders – pg. 168

Narrative
A strong ability in the skills of storytelling provide improvisers with the tools needed to create an evening of interesting improvised theatre and not be entirely reliant on

IMPORTANT CONCEPTS

games, quick jokes and gags. Everything is a narrative in the eyes of the audience and we must understand that as well as how to nurture and develop these narratives.

- Various Story Games - pg. 130-154
- What Comes Next - pg. 134-142
- Typing Game - pg. 151-154
- Word at a Time - pg. 114-115, 131-134, 329

While improvising it is a natural pitfall to avoid the dangerous or the unknown lying ahead by destroying stories. Directors and teachers need to be aware of how we avoid moving stories forward and encourage players to fearlessly continue.

A Story From Canada

Roman Danylo at the end of the show was playing in a DIE GAME to determine which team would win the evening match. After failing to continue his part of the story, he performed his solo death scene by getting hit by a car. The opposing player then ran on stage and gave him emergency surgery, dusted off his clothes and sent him on his way. The audience laughed and the next 5 minutes were spent with Roman ending his life while other performers from both sides saved his life. No one remembered the winner of the evening, only the playful 2nd place show finale.

Shawn Kinley, Calgary

TERMINOLOGY

Over the years Keith has developed terminology to pinpoint damage done to stories and resistance to learning. Here is an excerpt from one of Keith's newsletters defining the terms with an example of what they do to a story using Little Red Riding Hood to illustrate:

Keith Johnstone - Theatresports™ and Lifegame Newsletter - Issue Number 1, 1989

The show should present the whole variety of life.

Nadine Antler
Steife Brise, Hamburg, Germany

Cancelling:
Little Red Riding Hood was about to leave the house when Grannie phoned up and said 'Don't come'.

Sidetracking:
she set out with a basket of cookies and stopped to throw stones in the river. Soon a raft came by and she hopped on ... etc. (anything rather than meet the wolf)

Being Original:
(originality used as a way of sidetracking) – Little Red noticed something grey moving through the trees, at that moment she entered a time warp that took her back to the sixteenth century ...

Wimping:
This is usually a refusal to define i.e. Little Red met a big, huge, hairy, grey, friendly ... animal ... in the Forest (I swear improvisers will operate this way, removing the foundations of the story by refusing to identify the things they are interacting with).

Again! Productions - Paris, France
by *Romain Sablou*

Teatrul National Gagu, Mures, Romania by *Christina Ganj*

> Win or lose, the audience is your ultimate focus. A good natured dramatic loss gives the audience a better time than upset hurt egos. When the audience wins, you cannot lose.
> **Shawn Kinley**
> **Loose Moose Theatre**
> **Calgary, Canada**

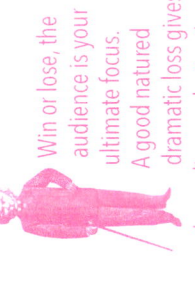

Conflict:
(when used to freeze action) "What big teeth you have Grandma?" "What's wrong with my teeth?"
"Well, they are big!"
"Let me see the mirror. My teeth are fine." "They're ugly."
"Rubbish."
And so on.

Instant Trouble (Instant Conflict):
Little Red stepped out of the front door and the Wolf gobbled her up.

Games (agreed activities):
Little Red gets to the cottage and she and Granny play table tennis all afternoon.

Hedging:
"Now you know Grannies' not been well, she lives on her own. I've told her it's silly but she won't listen. She's got arthritis, and it's difficult for her to look after herself…" And so on. Mum may never get to the point of actually giving Little Red the basket.

Gossip:
"Do you remember when I sent you with that basket of Cookies to Grannie?"
"Oh yes, I met the wolf!"
"Yes, that was before we had his head hung over the mantelpiece."
"I told him what big teeth he had."
"And he gobbled you up. The kettle's boiling. I'll make some Ovaltine."
"And it was a terrible shock to meet Grannie inside him."

Blocking:
"Are you going to see your Grannie, little girl?" "I don't have a Grannie!"

Negativity:
"All the better to gobble you up!"
"Oh well, if you must. God! Wolves are so boring." (this response is also a gag)

Gagging:
(see above) Little Red is a black belt and hurls the Wolf all over the room. i.e. she stays out of trouble.

As you probably realize, all of these techniques (perhaps with the exception of gagging) can be used to enhance a story instead of killing it. It's usually very clear when an improviser is working against narrative, and, with practice, easy to correct him.

THEATRESPORTS™ BY STEALTH

Keith Johnstone – Impro For Storytellers pg. 6/7

LET'S BEGIN

Let's say that students in an Impro scene are gabbing away and paying no attention to each other (because if they listened to what was being said they might be obliged to alter). You might slow them down by saying that the first student to use a word that includes an 's' loses the game; for example:

- 'Good morning, Dad.'
- 'You came in very late last night, Joan!'

Dad loses (because the word 'last' contains an 's'). Of course, if he'd been paying attention, he could have said something like: 'You came in very late . . . er . . . long after midnight, Joan!'

Students enjoy this game more if you split them into two teams and award the winner of each 'round' five points. They will now be playing a version of Theatresports™.

Add more games. Say that the first player to kill an idea loses, for example:- 'You seem out of breath. Been running?'
- 'It's my asthma . . .'

This asthma attack loses because it rejects the idea about running.

Or add a game in which you lose if you say anything that is not a question. - 'You want to interrogate me?'
- 'You're a suspect, aren't you?'
- 'Shall I sit down here?'
- 'That's my chair.' The suspect wins.

THE QUICK START

How to introduce Theatresports™ when meeting a class for the first time

1. Don't mention Theatresports™.
2. Teach a competitive game - the Hat Game would be perfect.
3. Suggest that they play it in two teams - three or four people in each team.
4. If the third stage was fun, add a Judge.
5. Add a Commentator.
6. Tell them that they're playing a simplified form of Theatresports™.
7. Ask two Team Captains to pick three or four players each. Appoint a scorekeeper, and three Judges. (EVENTUALLY)
8. Ask these teams to challenge to anything that occurs to them (at the discretion of the Judges); for example, to the best Master-servant scene or to an 'Indian leg-wrestle', or to the most frightening scene - whatever.

Impro Now
Adelaide, Australia
▪ by Tracey Davis

9. Encourage the onlookers to root for their teams and tremendous enthusiasm can be released.
10. Give each Judge a set of scorecards from one to five, and a bicycle horn that they can honk to end boring scenes.
11. Later on you can appoint the Commentator a microphone and you can appoint 'techies' (sound-and-lighting improvisers) and 'snoggers' (scenographers).

If you introduce the ideas piece by piece the students will feel that they thought up the game themselves. In good circumstances, competition generates a desire to improve technique, and the teacher becomes a resource for students who are eager to master the skills - an excellent teaching situation.

WHAT YOU NEED FOR BASIC THEATRESPORTS™

Improvisers
Three Judges
- A coin
- A horn – see page 34 of this manual for explanation
- A basket big enough for someone's head – see page 37 of this manual for explanation
- A set of scorecards. Cards should be large enough for people in the back row to see and numbered 1-2-3-4 and 5 on both sides of the card

A Commentator/Emcee/Moderator/Ombudsperson
- A microphone if needed

A Scorekeeper
- Scoreboard
- Pen or chalk or numbers to stick on and off

A performance space
- Stage, preferably with offstage and entrances, exits
- Place for teams and Judges
- Furniture, costumes, props for players and Snoggers – see page 42 of this manual for explanation

Lighting operator
- Lights on dimmers if possible

Sound operator/musician
- Audio equipment/computer and/or instruments

The opening shouldn't be too good. Make some mistakes.

Start the show comfortable. Connection is better than blind excitement.
Shawn Kinley
Loose Moose Theatre, Calgary, Canada

Keith Johnstone

A THEATRESPORTS™ SHOW

Keith describes a typical game (circa 1980).

Keith Johnstone - Impro For Storytellers pg. 2/3

Theatresports™ at Loose Moose

It's two minutes past eight on a Sunday evening and the smell of popcorn tells you that you're in the presence of something populist. The opening music starts, and the spectators begin to cheer as a follow-spot weaves over them. It settles on the Commentator, who stands in front of a scoreboard high up to the right of the semicircle of the audience.

He/she welcomes the spectators and breaks the ice, perhaps asking them to: 'Tell a stranger the vegetable that you most hate!' or 'Tell someone a secret you've never told anyone!' or 'Hug the stranger closest to you.' (I'm amazed that our spectators will agree to hug each other.)... The Commentator now becomes a disembodied voice that eases any difficulties, (and) explains the finer points. This voice can comment briefly without being intrusive, whereas emcees have to speak in paragraphs to make their interruptions seem worthwhile. 'Can we have the traditional boo for the Judges!' says the Commentator. This is a way of giving the audience permission to boo later on (should the urge take them).

Three robed Judges cross the stage to sit in the moat that surrounds our acting area. Bicycle horns hang around their necks (these are the 'rescue horns' used to honk boring players off the stage). Their demeanor is serious, it being less fun to boo light-hearted people.

On a typical night the Commentator might introduce: 'a ten-minute challenge match played by two of our rookie teams. Give the Aardvarks a big hand . . .'

Three or four improvisers scamper on from the side opposite their team bench. This allows us a view of them as they cross the stage. 'And now, a round of applause for the Bad Billys!' Teams should enter as a group, not as individuals, i.e. no 'stars' (too show-bizz.)

THE 10 MINUTE GAME

The Court Theatre - Christchurch, New Zealand
□ by Rachel Sears

The 10 Minute Game is a short challenge match with new improvisers. It is important for the host to mention that the players in the 10 Minute Game are new players. This takes stress off of them as the audience will adjust their expectations.

Benefits of the 10 minute game:

It gives newer players a short, safe and controlled experience on stage. Experience is the best instructor any performer could hope for.

It lowers the audience's expectations because, typically, the work of the newest performers is not going to be as strong as the improvisers who have been performing for 20 or more years.

It shows the audience that improvisation is not as easy as it looks.

It helps to ensure that the quality of the scene work will improve throughout the show.

The game can be played either as a Judge's Challenge Match where the Judges issue the challenges, which can be very useful for very new player, or a Challenge Match as described further on.

Keith Johnstone - Impro For Storytellers pg. 35

Behave like an athlete, think like an improviser.
**Nils Petter Morland
Det Andre Teatret,
Oslo, Norway**

'A judge and two team captains to the centre,' says the Commentator.

A coin is tossed, and perhaps the winner will create some benevolence by saying: 'You make the first challenge.'

A player crosses into 'enemy territory', and says: 'We, the Aardvarks, challenge you, the Bad Billys, to the best scene from a recent movie' (or whatever). 'We accept!' say their opponents.

Each team improvises their 'movie' scene (challengers going first), and the Judges award points by holding up cards that range from one to five; five means excellent, one means bad, and a honk from a rescue horn means 'kindly leave the stage'. Challenge follows challenge until an agreed time is reached.

Sometimes there are 'one-on-one' challenges, in which players from the opposing teams perform together - perhaps in a 'one-on-one love scene to be judged on sincerity and truth' (one-on-one scenes may involve several players from each team). Challenges can be to anything (at the discretion of the judges) - for example, Bruce McCulloch's challenge to 'the best scene completed in the length of time that I can submerge my head in a bucket of water'.

Teams add variety by challenging to scenes in mime, or in gibberish, or in verse, or in song, and so forth, while the Sound Imps (Sound Improvisers) supply thunder, or explosions, or blue-grass music, or 'The Ride of the Valkyries' or punk rock, or 'The Dance of the Sugar Plum Fairy', or 'vampire music', or love themes, or flushing toilets, or whatever else is appropriate.

This beginners' game is usually followed by a fifteen-minute Free-Impro in which a 'trainer' gives a class (exactly as I did with the Theatre Machine in the sixties).

THE FREE IMPRO

...a short class in training improvisers - especially those who were not able to get on a team, and to please the audience by letting them in on the secrets - the techniques - of the game - and can sometimes be the funniest part of the evening. (Explanations are minimal - in no sense is it a lecture. If the players understand, so will the audience - at least they will when they see the instructions applied.)

Keith Johnstone

The leader of the Free Impro session is a combination teacher in a workshop and zoo-keeper. The performers are happy monkeys who are eager to be on stage. (Sometimes a little effort is needed to keep them under control.) Remember, when the person leading the Free Impro asks, "can I have two people up" it's much nicer to see 5 people rush to the stage and send back three, than to stand there and beg for scared improvisers to step up. The attitude you show will reflect how the audience feels. 'Scared and nervous' or 'playful and happy'?

A Free Impro might include:
- Examples of Blocking and Accepting – and how enthusiasm affects the work.
- The attitude exercise to show how interesting it is for improvisers to have strong attitudes about the other characters. (see Impro For Storytellers pg. 233)
- Status exercises
- Mask work
- Examples of training exercises not often played in a match such as: Hands On Knees, Making Faces, Group "Yes!", Speaking in one Voice, etc.

The Free Impro can help improve the confidence of younger players. It is not meant to be used every night as if it was a scripted part of the show. Use it as a tool to benefit the needs of the show and to develop the audience and performers. You might be surprised how connected your audiences become when they are "let in" on the secrets.

Keith Johnstone

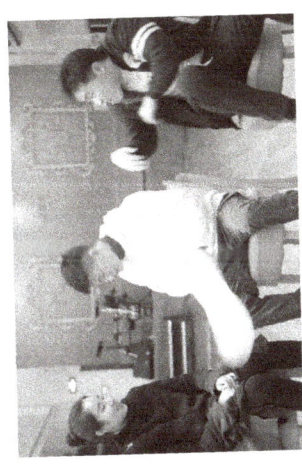

Beijing Horse Horse Tiger Tiger Culture Communication Inc. China ■ *by Zeng Cheng*

Allow the audience to be honest.

THE DANISH GAME

Keith suggests that groups begin their training with the Danish Game because it is easy to arrange and manage.

Keith Johnstone - Impro For Storytellers pg. 4/5

The Free-Impro is usually followed by a Danish Game (so called because I developed it in Denmark at a time when we wanted to emphasize the international appeal of Theatresports™).

The judges leave, and an 'Ombud' explains the penalty basket (if it hasn't already been used), and tells the spectators that after each pair of challenges they'll be asked to shout the name of the team that 'did the best scene'. He/she drills them into yelling as loudly as possible.

Some prissy Theatresports™ groups ask the audience to hold up colored cards to indicate the team they prefer, but that's gutless compared to shouting a team's name as loudly as you can.

LET'S BEGIN

After each pair of challenges, the 'Ombud' reminds the spectators of the scenes they've just been watching (because laughter interferes with transfer from the short-term memory). 'Did you prefer the love scene in which the Executioner eloped with the Prisoner? Or the love scene in which the aged Janitor said a tearful farewell to his broom? On the count of three - One! Two! Three!'

The winners earn five points, and a new challenge is issued. Sometimes there has to be a re-shout, and team names may have to be yelled separately, but even if we had a 'decibelometer' or whatever, we'd never use it. Yelling en masse is good for the soul.

The moderator (Ombudsman) always needs to adjust the names of the two teams to contain the same number of syllables, otherwise, when the audience shouts, the longest name has the advantage. 'Whooping' and whistling is discouraged because of the difficulty to hear everyone's choice.

Keith Johnstone

Remove the risk, the competition and the failure and you take the 'sport' out of Theatresports™

Loose Moose Theatre - Calgary, Canada
by Deborah Iozzi

THE REGULAR CHALLENGE MATCH

The Regular Challenge match is one team issuing a challenge and both teams playing a scene based on that challenge.
Team one challenges team two.
The challenging team always performs first.
Team one performs the challenge.
The other team sits offstage but in sight and considers a response (without being distracting to those on stage) that will add to the variety of the show.
Team one is scored.
Team two performs the challenge and is scored.
Team two then challenges team one. Again, the team issuing the challenge performs first.
Play continues for the duration of the match.
The Judges look to end on a good scene. This means that the overall time of the game is flexible.
The show concludes with the victor being announced and the teams crossing the stage to shake hands, like in a traditional team sporting event, waving to the audience and the commentator wishing everyone a good evening and safe drive home.

Keith Johnstone - Impro For Storytellers pg. 5/6

Our audience are out of the theatre by ten o'clock at the very latest, and if the performance has gone well, you'll feel that you've been watching a bunch of good-natured people who are wonderfully cooperative, and who aren't afraid to fail. It's therapeutic to be in such company, and to yell and cheer, and perhaps even go on stage with them.
With luck you'll feel as if you've been at a wonderful party; great parties don't depend on the amount of alcohol but on positive interactions.

VARIETY

Variety is very important in a Theatresports™ show. As a circus has the juggler before a death-defying act or as Shakespeare adds comedic characters to his darkest tragedies, so must improvisers struggle for diversity.

Improvisers need to be aware of adding variety because subconsciously players tend to fall into patterns and a whole evening is at risk of having the same style of content, themes or pace.

Look for variety in the following ways:

- Length of scenes – if one team does a long scene, answer with a short one
- Number of players on stage – if one team has a solo scene, do your scene with many players
- Visual look – if one team uses a blank stage, use furniture or lighting in your scene, or go into the audience
- Content – if one scene is a love scene, don't do another one
- Texture – if one scene is hilarious, follow it with something quiet, simple, slow, dramatic or silent
- Don't aim to make every scene funny, aim to tell stories

Keith Johnstone - Impro For Storytellers pg. 9/10

The Aardvarks leap onstage to present their scene.

'Wait!' I say: 'That's how the other team arrived. Isn't there some other way to express good nature and playfulness?'

They're baffled.

'Wish your colleagues good luck. Shake hands with them. Pretend they're boxers and that you're their seconds. Towel them. Mime putting gum-shields in their mouths. Announce them as the "Undefeated Winners" at this particular game. Let them sign autographs. You can't convey good nature, courage, affection and playfulness by being obedient!'

'But won't the Judges start to count us out?'

'I hope so [anything for variety] but when they do, just start the game!'

The Judges count out if the Team is being too slow. It shouldn't always happen.

In Europe the entire audience counts the players out before every scene. They should do it when the Judges do it. Sometimes a team needs more than 5 seconds and yet are not wasting time.

They are about to launch into their master-servant scene.

'Just a moment. There's a table and two chairs onstage, but that was the previous scenography. How about working on an empty stage? Or why not drag on the boat? Why not invite some audience members on to the stage and have them be distorting mirrors in a fun-fair.'

They remove the furniture while their team-mates sit in the moat and look bored.

'Whoa! Be eager to assist your colleagues [even if they're members of the other team]. This is theatre, not the work-a-day world where people are mean spirited and drag themselves about with "marks of woe".'

The Aardvarks begin their scene.

'Wait!'

'What now?'

'The other scene was set in a castle, and so is this one. Why not be two lighthouse keepers playing golf? Or God being massaged by one of the angels? Never repeat what the other team did unless they were so incompetent that you can say: "We'll show you how they should have played that scene!"'

THEATRESPORTS™ IN MORE DETAIL

DISASTER IS UNAVOIDABLE

The first time a group works in public they may be so humble, so vulnerable, that the audience's heart goes out to them. Next time, or the time after, they'll leap onstage without a trace of humility, and the audience will say to itself: 'So they think they're funny? Let's see them prove it!' and the glory turns to ashes. Yo-yoing between arrogance and humility when you're a beginner is as inevitable as falling off when you learn to ride a bike.

Keith Johnstone Impro For Storytellers pg. 12

Getting in front of an audience is important. Please don't hide and try to be perfect before you take the risk. Groups that train in private until they're highly skilled will hardly ever dare to venture into public; a pity because you learn quicker playing in front of unforgiving strangers than in front of forgiving friends.

Keith Johnstone

We need a bad scene right about now.

THE START OF THE SHOW

Fireworks and Fanfare….?

Some groups believe that there should be a great production at the beginning of their work to 'get the audience revved up". They want to create excitement and energy with a BIG beginning.

This approach can work against your improvisation by:
- Causing stress and anxiety in your players to 'live up to' the start
- Setting expectations of the audience with lots of performance values that they will not see through the rest of the evening in the improvised scenes, thus making an open blank stage seem like less
- Intimidating audience members and preventing them from participating as volunteers
- Creating a form of creative competition. Sometimes audience members can feel they need to 'live up to' the show with their suggestions. This makes it almost impossible to get honest, simple or truthful suggestions.

If the audience leaves feeling like the show was better at the beginning of the evening than the end or they are drained from the false enthusiasm, you will not see them returning week after week.

Start the show instead with the Commentator welcoming the audience and creating a positive environment that will support the improvisers as they step on stage to take risks.

Keith Johnstone

Most groups don't understand how competitive they are.

Society values perfection, success and safety. Theatresports™ values spontaneity, failure and risk.
Patti Stiles
Impro Melbourne, Australia

THE COMMENTATOR/EMCEE

(This is the preferred title instead of "Host". Their job is to introduce, clarify, maintain show efficiency and provide insights like a sports commentator would do. They are not there to entertain the audience.)

The Commentator's responsibilities are to:
- Be charming and efficient
- Explain what is happening in the show so the audience can relax and enjoy
- Introduce players and Judges
- Transition from one section of the show to another
- Help keep the teams and Judges on track (when needed) with who challenges next
- Announce what the Judges score each scene in case the audience can't see the cards
- Explain elements of the show for the audience Example: "The Horn will be sounded by the Judges when a scene is boring signaling players to leave the stage immediately. The performance is still scored."

It is very important that the Commentator is not competing with the players for laughs or attention.

Rapid Fire Theatre - Edmonton, Canada by Marc-Julien Objois

Keith Johnstone - Impro For Storytellers pg. 9

Let's say that the scene is over and the Judges are slow in giving their score - what does the Commentator do? "Tell them to hurry up? That's a bit high status. Say: "And the Judge's scores are . . ." If nothing happens, drop hints. Say quietly: "The Judges are taking their time over this decision ", or: "The audience are getting restive." Never seem bossy or aggressive.

Keith Johnstone - Impro For Storytellers pg. 23

COMPETITION

Some people (often fervent sports fans) condemn Theatresports™ on the grounds that it's competitive, but while 'straight' theatre encourages competition - and I could tell you stories that you'd hardly believe – Theatresports™ can take jealous and self-obsessed beginners and teach them to play games with good nature, and to fail gracefully.

It can be difficult for players to practically ignore the points that are being scored but it is imperative to "PLAY" the competition for the audience and know that you and the opposite team are working together to create good theatre for your audience.

Keith Johnstone

The teams at Loose Moose began to try to win at all costs, and even to screw-up the work of the other team. This was Sport on the model of, say, American football.

Theatresports™ became mean and aggressive - and the audience shrank heading for zero. I fixed this by having different teams each week. The teams still wanted to win but the players stopped attending to the score-board and began to have fun (instead of playing for the honor of their team). And then the audience came back again.

TEAMS

There is a difference between Impro and other forms of performance. One of the main ideas with Theatresports™ is that your partner is always there to support you (on stage and on the sidelines). Take care of each other. Make each other look good. If you are less concerned with yourself, you feel less fear and everyone wants to work with you.

Keith Johnstone

I attended a match where even the 'offstage' team was constantly onstage (being helpful to the other team'), and I was told that 'having everyone onstage is "democratic". Not so at Loose Moose where an experienced improviser will sometimes play against a four-person team.

'Wouldn't your audience love to see a solo performer thrust onstage and having to survive?'

'That would be "shining"!' they said. ('Shining' means showing off.)

'But it's thrilling to see a human being who is at the centre of attention, and who is without fear. Solo violinists, or magicians, or jugglers aren't shining!'

Arrogant players feel that they've failed if they're playing a submissive role, or are waiting on the bench. They leap onstage to share the glory whether they're needed or not, and yet the world's drama is based on scenes between two people. It's very difficult to find a good three-person acting scene because the third character is usually functioning as some sort of spectator - and why should improvisation be any different?

Scenes that involve all the players should be the exception, not the rule.

Patti Stiles - Impro Melbourne, Australia

TEAM ENTRANCES

I'm teaching Theatresports™ in class, and the Fat Cats and the Aardvarks are being introduced by a Commentator, and are crossing the stage to their team benches.

I interrupt: 'Don't struggle in like separate individuals. Be attentive to each other. Be visibly a group. Don't look isolated.'

They try again.

'Better!' I say. 'But you look nervous.'

Another attempt.

'Now you look arrogant. We preferred you the first time!'

'So what are we to do?'

'Keep imagining that the spectators are even nicer than you expected. Don't "demonstrate" this, just "experience" it, and trust that your positive feelings will be transmitted subliminally.'

Experience a little shock of pleasure each time you look out front.

Keith Johnstone - Impro For Storytellers pg. 7/8

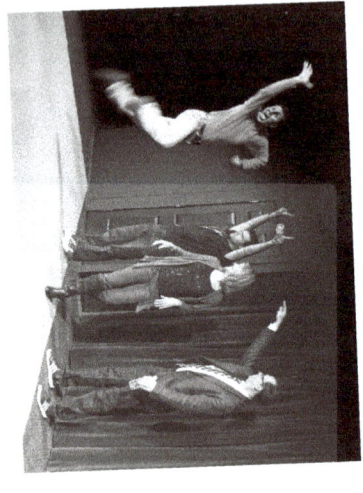

Loose Moose Theatre
Calgary, Canada
📷 *by Kate Ware*

I might ask them to imagine that they've been kept in a box full of wood-shavings all week, and that this is their one chance to be fully alive.

Or I might get them to enter with their eyes narrower than usual – this will almost certainly make them feel hostile - and then I'll try for the 'rebound' effect.

'Enter again, but this time let your eyes be wide open!'
Wide-eyed students see everything in a positive light, and huge energy can be released. They'll seem less afraid of the 'space' around them, and they're likely to stop 'judging themselves'. Remove defenses in life and you increase anxiety: remove them on-stage and anxiety diminishes.

Keith Johnstone - Impro For Storytellers pg. 3

SEATING TEAMS

Players should sit comfortably on benches at the side of the stage so as not to take attention from the performance but still be near enough to enter the stage quickly to help the other performers.

Teams at Loose Moose can sink into semi-obscurity in the two-foot deep moat around the stage, but many groups feature their teams, lighting them at all times, and sometimes sitting them across the rear of the stage, facing front, where they are forced to sustain fixed expressions of glee (this is typical of 'Game-Show Theatresports™', in which the emcee is the star and the players may be of no more consequence than the volunteers at 'give-away' shows on TV).

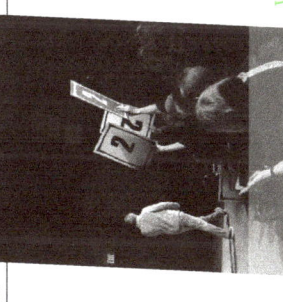

Loose Moose Theatre
Calgary, Canada
by Breanna Kennedy

LEAVING THE STAGE

When performers finish their scene, they should go to their bench.

Keith Johnstone

(Some performers want to take a bow for their performance but this becomes inefficient because the audience has likely applauded the work already as the lights have come down.)

JUDGES

Teatro a Molla - Bologna, Italy 📷 *by Gianluca Zaniboni*

Judges are not part of the entertainment, rather they are a vital element of the show structure with the role of protecting and supporting the players and improving the quality of the match. They are not just referees. Having the Judges looking after the players allows them to take bigger risks. You know the Judges will get you off stage if you are boring the audience, they will punish you if you offend the audience, they will keep you on track if you get distracted, they will make the tough call if needed and take the heat from the audience, protecting you and allowing the audience to view the player as the hero.

Keith Johnstone

The Judges are the firm parents, and the players are the 'naughty but good-natured children'.

Judges achieve all of this by:
- Being the authority figures that players and audiences can react to
- Adding efficiency and clarity
- Making decisions when needed
- Reminding players to issue and accept challenges efficiently
- Encouraging players to start scenes if stalling ("scene will begin in 5-4-3-2-1")
- Asking players to be louder
- Getting mediocre material off the stage before it bores the audience by:
  - Using The Horn
  - Waving down lights
  - Side-coaching "find an ending" or "30 seconds to end the scene."
- Keeping an eye on show content and variety:
- Warning players about behaviors that need to be addressed (Too much swearing, lack of variety in scene work, not starting scenes efficiently, etc.)

- Giving 'The Basket' penalty
- Rejecting challenges, just as the teams can - at their discretion to benefit the show. Examples - Rejection on the basis of being too repetitive "We have already seen that challenge", or too dangerous "Due to fire regulations no live flame is allowed on stage."

At the end of the scene, all Judges score between ONE (low) and FIVE (high).
Although all Judges are equal, there is one "Head Judge" whose title adds to the illusion of authority. He or she can referee the coin toss and also make final decisions.

▷ **TIP** - Judges should not wear funny costumes. This diminishes their role of authority in the eyes of the audience. It is more fun to yell at authority figures.

Don't give the Judges different responsibilities. For example a Narrative Judge, a Technical Judge, and an Entertainment Judge. We tried this and it never worked as intended. It was either ignored or caused confusion. Please don't do it.

Keith Johnstone

JUDGES ENTRANCE

Judges should not have elaborate entrances or interrupt the efficiency of the show. Judges should enter together and as they do the Commentator invites the audience to "Boo" them. This sets up the environment where the audience feels free to playfully respond to the authority figures of the show. Judges should not feel or act hurt by the booing.

Keith Johnstone - Impro For Storytellers pg. 8

I get the Commentator to say: 'Can we have the regulation "boo" for the Judges!' Two Judges cross the stage to their 'bench', while a third goes centre-stage to supervise the coin toss.

'You should all stay together,' I say.

'This saves time.'

'But then we don't see the Judges as "one organism".' Cross the stage as a unit and take your places while the audience hiss and boo.

Then the Commentator can cut into the booing by saying: "Head Judge to the centre for the coin toss, please!'" (This 'Head Judge' is a fiction – one Judge must not be able to boss the other two about.)

Performers who act as Judges must not be worried about the audience 'liking' them. Judging is a skill that needs to be learned. Players need to give their fellow players permission to make mistakes with the Horn and trust the Judges are there in the right spirit.

On a good night, the audience will react to the Judges when the Horn is sounded. Having the Judges booed is preferable to the players or the show being booed. A little emotion aimed at the Judges is also preferable to the audience going silent because no one is taking responsibility for the work on the stage.

⇨ **TIP** - Play games like the King Game in rehearsal to practice good Judge qualities.
(See IMPRO FOR STORYTELLERS pg. 237)

HELL JUDGES

Judges can be trained by using "Hell Judges". This is a unique way of getting performers to connect honestly to the needs of the audience. The Hell Judge (or judges) sits out of the audience's perception – usually behind them in the theatre. Their job is to watch the audience to see if they are engaged in the show, or not. Often the performers on stage and the Judges sitting in the loud front row can easily be influenced by the loud front row. This can mislead the Judges perspective on the entire audience.

When Hell Judges see that the audience is losing interest as a mass, they push a button that signals a light in front of the regular Judges. This signal is a small red light in view of the Judges and out of view of the audience. When the light goes on it is a STRONG indication that the Judges might want to sound the Horn for boring.

The Hell Judges light can help train the Judges as to when their impulses are in line with the audience and gives permission to use the Horn in case they were unsure.

Keith Johnstone - Impro For Storytellers pg. 67

Failure is part of any game, and unless this is understood, Theatresports™ will be a high- stress activity.

THE HORN

The Horn, referred to by many as the "Warning for Boring" is one of the most unique and important elements of Keith Johnstone's Theatresports™. "RESCUE HORN" implies a helpful tool to those in trouble. Imagine being on stage, your heart is pounding, the scene work is going poorly and your teammates off stage are covering their eyes, unable to watch the sinking ship you are on. If we play by the old rules of theatre, then the scene will drag on and eventually end. The audience will applaud politely and you will slink off stage knowing that the work was poor at best. But... this is Theatresports™, not traditional theatre. The Horn is sounded when the Judges deem a scene to be boring or is struggling and the players look stressed or unhappy. When the Horn is given, players get to run off stage without ego damage as the JUDGES take the blame for being "mean". Then we get to try again.

Keith Johnstone - Impro For Storytellers pg. 4

Scenes may drag, just as in conventional theatre, but anything tedious will be cut short by a 'Warning for Boring' (a honk from a rescue horn), and if the judges honk a scene that everyone is enjoying there'll be mass outrage.

Teatro a Molla - Bologna, Italy
by Manuel Nibale

The Horn protects players by allowing them to take risks and try new ideas, knowing that if it doesn't work the Judges will help get them off stage. It protects the audience from watching boring scenes and player's uninspired struggles. If the Judges horn a scene the audience was enjoying, then they get to yell, which brings great energy into the room and makes it more like a sporting event as when the Referee makes an unfair call against your beloved team.

In the past, Improvisers have yelled for weak judges to sound the Horn. They understand that it is not only there to aid them, but the audience as well. When everyone knows the work is going wrong, it is best to be honest and point it out. If we can do this in a good-natured way, we are connecting to the core of Theatresports™. The audience is seeing a special creature that can smile and play even in the face of failure. They are not capable of it themselves, but in doing this amazing thing, the audience will be entertained EVEN in failure. They can enjoy player success and failure because they have been given permission to, through good-natured behavior.

Keith Johnstone - Impro For Storytellers pg. 16/17/18

If a team receives a 'Warning for Boring' they have to end their scene and leave the stage (it's not a 'warning' but the real thing, but it sounds less insulting than a cry of 'booooorring'). 'Warnings' are given by a 'honk' of the rescue horn that each Judge wears around his/her neck. Before I bought these horns, 'warnings' were given by a zero card, but it feels less 'teachery' to be 'honked' off, rather than 'zeroed' off. (Judges can also end a scene by waving the lights down, as can the lighting operators or team members if they see a suitable moment.)

Even experienced players will plod on, hoping for inspiration that never comes. Our players will sometimes storm into our green room after a bad show saying: 'Where were the boring-calls when we needed them!' (as if forbidden to end boring scenes themselves).

selves), but there is a minority of players who so enjoy being the centre of attention that they don't care if they're tedious. I heard one say: 'I'm a performer – why should I care what the audience think?' (making me wonder about his sex life).

Such players will complain that the warning is being given (or that the lights are fading), before people have lost interest, but could there possibly be a better time? The audience will howl with rage if a scene is honked unjustifiably, and this unites them with the actors against the Judges (good!), and yet selfish players will resent the 'injustice'.

'No Judge can be right all the time,' I say. 'And Theatresports™ is not a school where everyone's prestige depends on being marked correctly. After all, you're not being cast out into the tundra during a blizzard.'

'But don't you realize what a depressing effect the warning has on the audience?'

'It does if the players skulk off like whipped dogs, but it's heart-warming to see improvisers who are thrown off and stay good natured.'

'If you want to be dignified, why improvise? Handled ineptly, warnings can be brutal, but used properly they create benevolence. The spectators adore improvisers who can be thrown offstage and yet stay happy.

Accepting the Warning.

At least one group softens the warning by saying that it just means 'that the players failed to see a possible ending'. This goes against the nature of sport. The spectators want to see boxers being knocked out, speed-boats flipping over, and improvisers being told unequivocally that their scene has failed. Boring means boring and many scenes are boring after twenty seconds (already irredeemably stupid).

Instead of learning how to be rejected with good humor – which can take all of five minutes – many groups remove the warning.

Another unsatisfactory solution is to impose time limits on all scenes, sometimes as little as one or two minutes ('unsatisfactory' because players should learn how to end scenes by themselves). I've even heard of Theatresports™ being advertised as 'no scene over ninety seconds', which might make some sense if the entire event only lasted for fifteen minutes, but why kill scenes that have a lot of power and energy? Perhaps weak judges had allowed boring scenes to drag on pointlessly, and the ninety-second rule was an act of desperation.

In the early days we were so protective of the players' feelings that a team kept possession of the stage until the third warning, and all warnings had to be unanimous. Then we threw teams off after the second warning. Finally, after much heart-searching, we decided that justice was less important than getting dead scenes off the stage, and we said that any Judge could end any scene at any time (without consultation), but even then dreary scenes were sometimes allowed to continue while the bored Judges toyed with their rescue horns but were reluctant to 'do the deed'.

These days the so-called Hell-Judges (improvisers who are sitting at the rear of the audience, see p. 324) can press a button when they're bored. This flashes a red 'Hell light' at the Judges' feet, and in the lighting booth. The official Judges can ignore this, but it's likely to shake them out of their apathy.

I could have invented more discrete ways to remove improvisers from the stage - as in 'comedy lounges' where the comedian has to leave when a picture lights up behind the bar - but I wanted the warnings to be blatant because I was tired of the audience that 'appreciates' theatre and says, 'I quite liked it', as if discussing a dubious egg.

THEATRESPORTS™ IN MORE DETAIL

This concept is really quite advanced. Teachers who had bad training themselves miss the point. They learned to avoid failure rather than incorporate and deal with it in a healthy way. Perhaps not surprisingly, young people have an easier time than many adults in dealing with the Horn, the Basket and failure in general.

If a team is 'honked off the stage, make sure that they stay good natured. Professional actors are very likely to express anger or resentment, but no one admires this, or wants to invite them home after the game.

Keith Johnstone Impro For Storytellers pg. 11

An exercise to teach happy failure with the Horn

>> When I teach people the Horn I use this little exercise I came up with. I ask three people to be Judges and ask everyone else to go to one side of the stage. I tell them: "In pairs you will come out and play a scene. At some random point the Horn will go. Let's practice receiving the Horn with a playful good natured response. Look happy after you hear the Horn. If you look annoyed or pissed off, you'll have another go or as many goes as is needed because sometimes we don't realise our own expressions and how the audience perceives them." Then I will sit behind the three Judges and I might tap one or all three of them to horn the scene to help encourage the randomness of response. Two players come to the stage, at some point we horn, if they look happy I say "thank you, next!" and two more players come onto the stage. If they don't look happy I'll say "you looked a bit pissed off, or startled or annoyed. Try again!" Then they do another scene. I aim to make the horns random and playful. I look for moments when they think it won't happen because that is when we get the real honest expression. I let some scenes go long, horn some people walking on, after an opening line, or let it drag till they wish there was one. If the three Judges are doing a good job, I don't interrupt. I'm there to take the pressure off and to support them.

Often people become very aware of the difference between a playful acceptance of the Horn and a negative one. They also learn that giving the Horn is not always easy and have more understanding for the Judges.
I then build this into moving away from the random and looking for the moment to horn to save the players. Teaching Word At A Time with 'Again!' is a nice lead in to the above exercise. << Patti Stiles

Impro Melbourne - Australia ▫ by Mak Gambino

Courtyard Playhouse - Dubai, UAE ▫ by Tiffany Schultz

Impro Okinawa - Japan ▫ by Kudaka Tomoaki

THE BASKET

The Judges can penalize players by sending them briefly out of play with a basket on their head for 2 minutes (typically sent to the shadows where they could be seen by the audience if they want but will not be distracting to the stage work). While the punishment is merely representational, it adds to the mock authority and importance of the competition. It also supports the players by allowing them to play without creative censorship.

Should they say or do something that could be seen as poor taste, they are punished. By applying this penalty the audience feels the offending player has been dealt with and any potential awkwardness has been avoided.

The Basket penalty is typically awarded to a player who is "rude, crude or offensive" **outside the context of the scene**. The Judges often bend this suggestion to suit the moment. For example, a player who has continually misbehaved at the Judge's expense would be awarded a basket. In one very rare instance an audience member was given a basket for something he said. Another member of the audience actually called for the basket! It was in good nature and added to the evening's experience.

The audience is often invited to call out for baskets. They like it and it adds direct involvement. But if you incorporate this into your performance, make it clear that a call for basket should come AFTER the scene has been completed.

Some groups invite their audience to yell and throw things during the scene work. This encourages silliness and the chance of something worthwhile being achieved under such circumstances is just about zero. Such distraction calls more attention to the structure than to the actual scene work. It can also be dangerous to throw objects at players as they have lights in their eyes and may not see the incoming projectile.

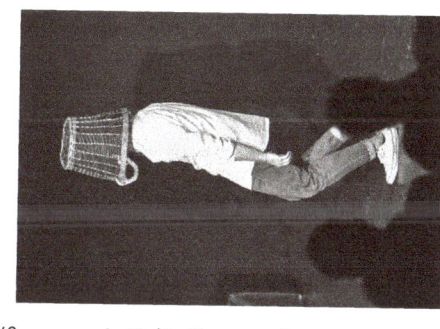

Theater Anundpfirsich
Zurich, Switzerland, by *Mike Hamm*

SCORING AND SCORECARDS

In judged matches, each judge sits with five large cards (approximately knee high – big enough to be seen at the back of the theatre.) Each card has a large number on it. They are numbered ONE to FIVE on both sides of the card. Immediately following the scene, the Judges raise their Score-card for the audience and Commentator (and Scorekeeper) to see. The scores are added up and put on the scoreboard.

Quadrifolli
Milano, Italy
by *Gippo Morales*

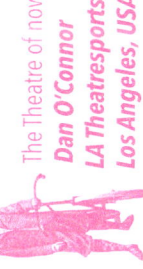

The Theatre of now.
Dan O'Connor
LA Theatresports™
Los Angeles, USA

Keith Johnstone Impro For Storytellers pg. 10

'Let's imagine that the Aardvarks have performed an uninspired scene. Will the judges please score it.' Each Judge holds up a one (point) card.

'But if the scene was only worth a one, why were we watching it? Honk boring players off the stage. Don't let them burble on.'

THEATRESPORTS™ IN MORE DETAIL

Even if the scene is horned off the stage, it is still scored by the Judges. This is another chance for the audience to show their outrage if they disagree with the Judges or yell enthusiastically when "their" team gets the score they deserve.

In the case of a ONE on ONE or a TEAM on TEAM challenge, the Judges each raise one arm and point one finger in the air. Then at the same time, they point to the team that each of them believe won that challenge.

Scoring for a Danish match involves the audience cheering for the team whose scene they like best at the end of a round. After both teams have answered the challenge with their scene, the Moderator asks the audience to yell the name of the team they prefer. The winning team is awarded 5 points.

Keith Johnstone - Impro For Storytellers pg. 9

I ask them to imagine that the Fat Cats have performed well. Each Judge holds up a three card. 'But if it went well - why not a couple of fours? Don't be afraid to be criticized for scoring high!'

FAIRNESS

In some groups around the world, Judges will often try to score scenes in a way that the points are 'balanced'. The idea that teams should earn equal points regardless of the entertainment value of the work goes against the idea of honesty in improvisation.

When Judges try to create drama by altering the score artificially, the audience is aware and feels manipulated. When the audience sees a vastly superior team in a tie with a team that has struggled all night, they feel cheated. The improvisers will also likely feel hidden shame after tying (or worse winning) against a stronger team.

It's not about making things 'fair and balanced'. It is more important to train players to retain a positive state of mind and deal with failure or loss (and equally with success and winning).

CHALLENGES

Loose Moose Theatre
Calgary, Canada
📷 *by Breana Kennedy*

⊃ **TIP** - Simple efficiency is a theme that Keith encourages. Practice setting up your scene or game using as few words as necessary and get on with the performance.

Much discussion goes into what makes a good challenge and which challenges will best benefit a show. Remember that Theatresports™ is a performance filled with variety. If every scene were a specified time and similar emotional quality, the show would not draw an audience week after week. Here's what Keith suggests:

Keith Johnstone - Impro For Storytellers pg. 13-16

Issuing challenges: Keep a certain formality. Challenges should seem important. (If the players can't take the game seriously why should the onlookers?) And be brief. Most challenges are self explanatory. If you neglect something essential - for example, that a 'miss-grab' loses a Hat Game - the Commentator or a Judge can clarify this. ➔

Many teams only challenge to games (and to the same games), but unexpected and unheard-of challenges keep the players alert. Challenge to novelties like a spelling-bee, or to the most convincing impersonation of a celebrity, or to the best scene with an audience member, or to the best scene directed by the other team. Take risks. Challenges that seem stupid, incomprehensible or repetitive must always be rejected (at the discretion of the Judges).

A team can say: We object!" and the Judges can ask: "On what grounds?" They can then say: "Overruled!" or: "Sustained!"

Some groups want to ban challenges that 'always fail' (there was once a move to veto the He Said/She Said Game, but if we avoided every game that a group disliked, the difficult ones would never be mastered. The problem lies not in the games, but in weak judges who let uninspired scenes drag on. If the players are boring (which they will be if they're screwing up a game), throw them off.

Great teams brain-storm to find new challenges; for example: to the best one-minute radio drama played in the dark (this gives our audience a chance to cuddle), to the best scene featuring an object chosen by the other team (at the Olympics, Calgary offered a live goat), to the best scene using an audience volunteer (off-limits to beginners because volunteers must be treated with love and generosity and this takes skill), to the best enactment of a folk tale (with an audience volunteer as the Hero), to the best love scene with a tragic ending, to the best excuse, to the best lie, to the best exposure of an injustice, to the best revenge, to the best escape, to the most compassionate scene, to the best use of the other team (e.g., as a blob in a science-fiction movie, as furniture, as bowling balls), to the most serious, positive, truthful, romantic, horrific, or boring scene (the Danes at the Olympics presented an unforgettable 'most boring consummation of a marriage'), to a family relationship, to a scene with pathos, and so on.

Great teams set themselves goals like including audience volunteers in every scene, or playing each scene in gibbberish. When teams only challenge to Theatre Games (and to the same games week after week) this creates the same monotony as soup followed by soup followed by soup.

Games are for providing contrast, and should be interspersed between stories, or between challenges to 'the best religious scene', or 'to the most psychotic scene', or whatever.

The need for variety: Wonderful challenges are sometimes created in the heat of the moment, but when inspiration fails, each challenge is likely to resemble the one before. A scene in which someone asks for a job is followed by another scene in which someone asks for a job. Some groups try to solve this by issuing vague challenges; for example: "We challenge you to a scene involving physical skills", but then Theatresports™ moves further away from sport (because there's less direct comparison between the teams).

The Audience team would avoid such problems by shouting: 'The book! The book!' in pretended panic, and run to open a book in which they had written possible challenges. If you create such a book, write verbal challenges in one column, physical challenges in another, solo challenges in another, and so on.

Duration of challenges: Some groups expect every scene to last for six minutes (or whatever), but this diminishes variety. Others assume that a scene that lasts a quarter of an hour is better than one that lasts thirty seconds. I've seen matches in which not one scene pleased the performers, and yet they struggled to make them all last for at least six minutes. It would have been better to say: 'This is garbage! Can we start again!'

Avoid 'lock-ins': Don't trap yourself by announcing what will happen unless you have to. For example: if the Commentator has said:

THEATRESPORTS™ IN MORE DETAIL

'And now for the final challenge', and the scenes are dreary, it becomes difficult for the Judges to add a further challenge. Another example: a Director set up a dramatic scene, and over-directed it by saying: 'You can only use three word sentences.' It would have been better to add this instruction later in the scene - If it was needed.

Baulking: A challenge can be baulked at (refused) at the discretion of the Judges. Such baulks add variety and give the spectators something to discuss on the way home. Typical baulks might be: 'We want to baulk at that challenge on the grounds that every-one's sick of it!' Or: 'We think that challenge is too vague.' Or: 'We'd like to baulk unless they can make us understand what they mean!' Or: 'We've just had two scenes in verse. Does anyone really want them to be followed by two singing scenes?' If a baulk is upheld, a fresh challenge must be issued, and if this should also prove unacceptable, the Judges must issue a challenge of their own.

Judges can also baulk. They can say: 'We object to that game!' (and give reasons), or they can drop hints, for example: 'If you'd like to baulk at that we'll be delighted to uphold you!'

Baulks should never be accepted automatically; for example: 'We challenge you to the best scene involving a beard!'

'We baulk at that!'

'On what grounds?'

'On the grounds that they've got beards and we haven't!'

'Overruled!'

Correct! After all, a clean-shaven team could improvise beards from wigs, or a scientist could invent a hair-restorer so powerful that a SWAT team has to shave its way into him.

When three members of a team were sitting with their heads in penalty baskets (a rare occurrence), the fourth player baulked at a challenge to: 'the best four-person pecking-order'. This was overruled on the grounds that the audience would be delighted to see one person play four different characters (or working with three audience volunteers).

Players wishing to be cooperative will agree to be in scenes that hold not the slightest interest for them (or for us), but it's better to baulk than to collude in mutual self destruction.

Keith Johnstone - Impro For Storytellers pg. 8

While the other team is playing, don't spend all your time whispering to each other about how you are going to respond. Watch their scene with shining eyes and trust someone to jump up and announce to the audience what form your response will take.

Tom Salinsky - The Spontaneity Shop, London, England

The Fat Cats win the toss, and one of them mumbles: 'What about a master-servant scene?' I cut in: 'You're young, you're healthy, you aren't crippled! Stride to the other half of the stage and hurl your challenge in a clear voice. Be formal; announce: "We, the Fat Cats, challenge you, the Aardvarks, to the best master-servant scene!" The voice is not just to be heard, it's a whip that disciplines the spectators. Be dynamic! Forget this Hamlet stuff of feeling queasy before the duel!'

WINNING PRIZES

When creating Theatresports™ events be very careful about awarding prizes to the winners. Originally, Theatresports™ festivals offered trophies made of found objects around the theatre.

Keith's thoughts were that the prize should be inconsequential and not add to the instinct to make the competition real. He even told festival attendees that they should all go to their home theatres and announce that they had all won and the host theatre should always confirm the information when press and media called from their city. The focus of the show should be working together to inspire each other and create an evening the audience will remember. If you add prizes it will increase actual competition and begin to unravel the spirit of good-natured play and teamwork.

✳ A Story From Norway

In Norway, the national improvisation festival that claimed to crown the best young improvisation team in the country offered thousand-dollar scholarships to the winners. For years, the festival was known for some of the least inspired work and poor spirit. Teams took the competition seriously and good nature was scarce. These days the festival has a new outlook. They still offer a scholarship, but now the jury considers other criteria. Today they look at supportiveness in the games, how the groups work together, where they come from and who would benefit most from the money. They may even split the prize between deserving players or groups. — Helena Abrahamsen, Oslo

✳

KEITH'S ADVICE

So my advice is:
- Find Judges who will throw you off when you're boring.
- Play a match in public before you know what you're doing.
- Keep the first matches mercifully short (ten minutes is ample and can seem like hours when you are uninspired).
- Screw-up with good humor.
- 'Lick your wounds'; practice the skills; plunge in again.
- In a school context, performing in public may mean playing in front of another class, or during the lunch-hour, or challenging another school.

Keith Johnstone - Impro For Storytellers pg. 12

Steife Brise - Hamburg, Germany
📷 by Klaus Friese

Loose Moose Theatre Calgary, Canada 📷 by Deborah Iozzi

Loose Moose Theatre - Calgary, Canada
📷 by Deborah Iozzi

ATTENTION TO DETAIL

SCENOGRAPHY

Not exclusively for Theatresports™, Scenography is the art of supporting players and their scenes by enhancing the environment with props, furniture, cloth material and other objects. Even if there is no substantial Scenography or Scenographers to animate it, it is good to have some props, hats, clothing, long balloons, etc. available to the improvisers.

Loose Moose Theatre Calgary, Canada
📷 *by Kate Ware*

At the Loose Moose Theatre, Scenography developed greater relevance with improvisers Tom Lamb and Shawn Kinley who took the technical aspect of moving furniture for efficiency and transformed it into creating vivid images with simple objects found backstage. Shawn mentioned, *"We felt good when we saw the improvisers light up with inspiration because of something we offered."*

Scenography is a strong teacher of improvisation. The Scenographer is always looking for ways to support the scene and the players or to enhance the show. These are useful skills for any improviser.

Not every theatre group or company has access to a wide array of props so workshops have been developed around adapting Scenography to the available tools at hand.

Here are some ideas:

Practice "Scenography in a suitcase". (A simple case or box full of collapsible and adaptable objects can make it look like you have 10 times more props than you actually have. (Solid colored material becomes a cape, screen, river, etc., umbrellas become trees, radar dishes, etc..). You don't need much storage space for a suitcase of well-chosen props.

Develop mime skills and use your bodies to become the necessary objects and characters.

Practice adapting your available environment into other realities.

Here are some examples of Scenographic support:
- Create a living room or office when the scene calls for it (three chairs covered with a blanket as a sofa, a box for a table if no table is available, etc.).
- Add the extra characters that can embellish a restaurant or archaeological dig.
- Make people fly by simply lifting them.
- Alter the physical perspective of the scene to enhance the narrative by creating a tiny village with fingers for monsters to trample.

Play Theatresports™ the way Keith intended it.
Dennis Cahill - Loose Moose Theatre Calgary, Canada

Keith Johnstone - Impro For Storytellers pg. 5

Whenever possible I surround the players with tables covered with junk - a golf-cart, beds and bedding, wheelchairs, a boat that they can 'row' about the stage, and whatever. On tour the Theatre Machine used to raid the prop rooms - borrowing, for example, the massive Hansel and Gretel's cage from the Vienna Opera (and then not using it).

'Scenographies' are supplied by 'Snoggers', who lurk backstage ready to roll tumbleweed across the stage for a Western scene, or to drape chairs with 'mylar' for a scene in heaven. They'll fold back the carpet to reveal the taped outline of a body (to establish a crime scene), or lay a black-painted ladder on the stage to indicate a 'railroad track', or they'll stand on opposite sides of the stage holding up baskets to establish a gymnasium. Audience volunteers are sometimes conscripted: I once saw fifty people run on to the stage and lie down and make sucking noises while the improvisers pretended to be duck hunters wading through a swamp.

NOTES

After a performance, Keith would often give notes about the show. Notes are an important source of information for players about the show and their individual performance.

The notes are about both the scenes and the show in general. Points of focus could be:
- Could players be heard?
- Was there ample variety in the show or were there three scenes in a row about going on a date?
- Were players in the light?
- Did a scene follow through on the promises in the platform, or did it stall?
- Did Judges take enough risks with the Horn?
- Did players treat audience volunteers well? ...And so on.

Try this:
- After a show sit together.
- Review a list of the scenes and technical elements.
- Share brief feedback but don't discuss.
- Have a director who can reference individual performer's success or failure on stage with a view to educating that performer, and their colleagues. Example: If someone is shining or controlling scenes, this must be part of the show notes. Otherwise the session becomes just a review of the show without development. This is missing from many Theatresports™ groups and potentially holds back their development.

Understand that you are going to hear one person's point of view about the show. This does not mean the notes offered are right or wrong, just an opinion. Notes are given simply, efficiently and with no discussion. They should focus on what happened, not what a player 'wishes' would have happened. Comments should be worded to provide information and perspective, not to accuse or blame but to point out how the scene work either failed or succeeded. A 15 minute note sessions is all you need for a two hour show.

Have someone in charge sit in front and "lead" the session. Move it forward when necessary. Discuss the notes anywhere any time - but not during the note session. It takes too long and can generate bad feelings.

Receiving Notes

Some people react as though their egos have been crushed but most quickly understand that the notes are meant to improve the shows and one's own development. REMEMBER the notes are meant to better the future work. They are about the work and not the person.

Sketch by Keith Johnstone

Teatro A Molla - Bologna, Italy by Gianluca Zaniboni

Stage Heroes - Singapore
 by Hyperfrontal Productions

Det Andre Teatret - Oslo, Norway by Nils Peter Mørland

GAMES LIST

IMPRO FOR STORYTELLERS contains games and exercises useful in the development of improvisation skills, storytelling and the spirit behind Theatresports™.

We recommend getting Keith's book and using the following exercises:

- Giving Presents *pg. 58 training*
- Word-at-a-Time *pg. 131 training & performance*
- What Comes Next? *pg. 134 training & performance*
- Three-word Sentences *pg. 155 training & performance*
- One-word Sentences *pg. 155 training & performance*
- The Hat Game *pg. 156 training & performance*
- Making Faces *pg. 162 training & performance*
- Dubbing *pg. 177 training & performance*
- The Die Game *pg. 183 training & performance*
- Endowments *pg. 185 training & performance*
- Freeze Games *pg. 186 training & performance*
- Guess the Phrase *pg. 187 training & performance*
- The No 'S' Game *pg. 188 training & performance*
- A Scene Without... *pg. 189 training & performance*
- Sideways Scenes *pg. 189 training & performance*
- Yes-But *pg. 190 training*
- Justify the Gesture *pg. 193 training*
- He Said/She Said *pg. 195 training & performance*
- Moving Bodies *pg. 200 training & performance*
- The Arms *pg. 202 training & performance*
- Sound Scape *pg. 208 training & performance*
- Boring the Audience *pg. 211 training & performance*
- Wallpaper Drama *pg. 212 training & performance*
- Gibberish *pg. 214 training & performance*
- Status *pg. 219 training & performance*
- Party Endowments *pg. 233 training & performance*
- The King Game *pg. 237 training & performance*
- Master-Servant *pg. 240 training & performance*
- Slow-motion Commentary *pg. 241 training & performance*

Unexpected Productions, Seattle, USA

In teaching the format, some instructors might be tempted to teach students that the GAMES are Theatresports™. This is far from true. Games are used to adjust behavior that is detrimental to the success of the performers and their scene work.

Games can be fun and also benefit the growth of the player. When the lesson has made an impact, it's easier for the players to remove the structural safety and take more risk.

There are many different games, some much more useful than others. Useful games train improvisers in supportive, benevolent behavior and to embrace risk and failure. Useful games also train storytelling skills. Less useful are the games that train improvisers in bad habits like disconnection from each other and damaging stories. Beware of games that are merely verbal or intellectual acrobatics, or that encourage competition and bad feelings. The audience may be laughing but ask yourself "why?". Check that all players are enjoying the experience.

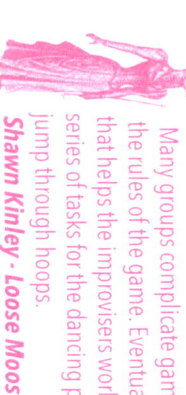

Many groups complicate games because they get good at the rules of the game. Eventually a simple and elegant game that helps the improvisers work better becomes a complicated series of tasks for the dancing poodles to perform with as they jump through hoops.

Shawn Kinley - Loose Moose Theatre, Calgary, Canada

Courtyard Playhouse - Dubai, UAE by Tiffany Schultz

IN CLOSING

FINAL WORDS

Theatresports™ was born out of a desire to have fully engaged audiences at a public theatre event. That vision, however, was never the main goal. As the concept grew and developed, it became clear that to have any lasting value, our lives and the audience's own experiences would need to be reflected in the scenes. The scenes need to be the substance of a Theatresports™ show.

When played properly, it is evident that the content is more important than the package. Precisely because Theatresports™ is such a grand participatory ritual, we should strive to focus extra attention on the stories being told amidst the fanfare. The joyful absurdity of cheering for make-believe teams in a staged event can be beautifully offset by scenes with poignancy and honest emotion.

Once the atmosphere has been boisterous, the quiet moments have more meaning. When you get them laughing, then there's a chance to pull heartstrings, draw tears or simply have them listen.

Harlekin Theatre - Tübingen, Germany 📷 by Hartmut Wimmer

A Story From Japan

 Members from several groups around the country were having a Theatresports™ weekend workshop with a public show to follow.

The last scene of the evening was a team-on-team tie-breaker. Whereas in many countries a possible game choice is a Rhyming Scene, because of the grammar, that concept doesn't work in Japanese. Instead they played "Best scene speaking in Haiku." The result was so poignant and pleasing that the audience could be heard sighing and gasping, the players were visibly shaken and even those who didn't understand the language felt as if they had witnessed something simple yet splendid.

Steve Jarand

Welcome to the ITI community and best of luck in your adventures with Theatresports™!

FOR MORE INFORMATION:

Impro (Methuen) - Keith Johnstone
Describes the genesis and ongoing development of Impro Theatre.

Impro For Storytellers (Faber and Faber) Keith Johnstone
Describes the Theatresports™ format, background and essential points about how to play. Other KJ formats as well as many scenes/games/exercises are also explained.

ITI Newsletters
This is a monthly online publication to share articles, resources and stories.
sign up at theatresports.org/iti-newsletter

Theatresports.com
On the "Resources" tab - Keith Johnstone Newsletters (password protected). There are several dedicated entirely to Theatresports™.
Also found there are: recommended teacher's list, videos, books, articles, format guides and translations.

Theatresports™ Handbook APP
available on iTunes

For Direct Questions:
admin@theatresports.org
Or better yet, contact your regional representative.
theatresports.org/board-members-contact-us

www.ingramcontent.com/pod-product-compliance
Lightning Source LLC
Chambersburg PA
CBHW061936290426
44113CB00025B/2934